~ Cheryl ~
A GIFT FOR

~ Janell ~
FROM

Cheryl~
May you have the spirit of Christmas which is Peace, the gladness of Christmas which is Hope, and the Heart of Christmas which is Love! much love,
Janell

- 2017 -

Copyright © 2016 Hallmark Licensing, LLC

All scripture taken from the HOLY BIBLE: NEW INTERNATIONAL VERSION®. NIV®. Copyright © 1973, 1978, 1984 by International Bible Society. Used by permission of Zondervan.

Published by Hallmark Gift Books,
a division of Hallmark Cards, Inc.,
Kansas City, MO 64141
Visit us on the Web at Hallmark.com.

All rights reserved. No part of this publication may be reproduced, transmitted, or stored in any form or by any means without the prior written permission of the publisher.

Editorial Director: Delia Berrigan
Editor: Kim Schworm Acosta
Art Director: Chris Opheim
Designer: Laura Elsenraat
Production Designer: Dan Horton

ISBN: 978-1-63059-009-3
XKT1697

Made in China
0417

A Journey of Faith, Hope, and Love

VOICES AND BLESSINGS FROM THE NATIVITY STORY

Story from the Gospels of Matthew and Luke

Blessings and Voices by Paige DeRuyscher

Featuring the art of Matt Kesler

Introduction

Every day, Jesus Christ brings hope and meaning to my life. The story of His birth has always been something my family holds as a miraculous, powerful event in history.

It also has played a significant role in my nearly 30 years as a professional artist. I began creating religious Christmas illustrations at Hallmark Cards because I felt a lot of existing imagery lacked a true sense of emotional connection. Also, the births of our children were such sacred experiences for my wife and me that I wanted to capture the wonder of Christ's birth—both the humanity and the sacredness—in a very real way.

Along the way, I met writer Paige DeRuyscher, a kindred spirit. She joined my quest to bring new life to this wonderful story through art, scripture, blessings, and the voices of Mary, Joseph, and others as we might imagine them.

Our aim is to honor scripture while bringing color and authenticity to those who took this journey. We invite you to experience this book in your own way and find lasting hope within its pages.

Merry Christmas to you and yours,
Matt Kesler

During the time of King Herod, a virgin from Nazareth was pledged to be married to a man named Joseph, a descendant of David. The virgin's name was Mary.

God sent the angel Gabriel to Mary.

The angel said, *"Greetings, you who are highly favored! The Lord is with you."*

Mary was greatly troubled at his words and wondered what kind of greeting this might be.

{MARY}

Who will believe this story?
That a messenger of God
would appear here, in my house,
to speak to me of carrying this child...
the One that the world awaits?
How is it possible?
I am a daughter, a sister...
I am no man's wife.
What will happen to me?

But the angel said to her, *"Do not be afraid, Mary;*

you have found favor with God. You will conceive and give birth

to a son, and you are to call him Jesus. He will be great and will be

called the Son of the Most High. The Lord God will give him the throne

of his father David, and he will reign over Jacob's descendants forever;

his kingdom will never end."

A CHRISTMAS BLESSING FOR YOU: *Peace*

Mary knew the fear of uncertainty.
She encountered the unexpected
and lived with the unknown.

"Do not be afraid," the angel said.

And God speaks those words
into our lives again and again.

May His presence bring you peace
that's deeper than your fears,
stronger than your doubts,
greater than any challenge
life brings you.

At that time Mary got ready and hurried to a town in the hill country of Judea, where she came to Zechariah's home and greeted Elizabeth. When Elizabeth heard Mary's greeting, the baby leaped in her womb, and Elizabeth was filled with the Holy Spirit.

In a loud voice Elizabeth exclaimed: *"Blessed are you among women, and blessed is the child you will bear! But why am I so favored, that the mother of my Lord should come to me? As soon as the sound of your greeting reached my ears, the baby in my womb leaped for joy. Blessed is she who has believed that the Lord would fulfill his promises to her!"*

And Mary said, "*My soul glorifies the Lord and my spirit rejoices in God my Savior, for he has been mindful of the humble state of his servant. From now on all generations will call me blessed, for the Mighty One has done great things for me—holy is his name.*"

A CHRISTMAS BLESSING FOR YOU: *Connection*

What a gift it is to be truly understood.
When someone sees not only who we are
but who we are becoming,
our spirit rejoices in being known.

Elizabeth believed in Mary
and in what God could do through her.
She spoke life into Mary's fearful heart
and calmed her restless spirit.

May you, too, feel the happiness and comfort
of being seen and known by others,
just as Christ sees and knows you . . .
all you are today and all you will become.

Because Joseph her husband was faithful to the law and yet did not want to expose Mary to public disgrace, he had in mind to divorce her quietly. But after he had considered this, an angel of the Lord appeared to Joseph in a dream and said,

"Joseph son of David, do not be afraid to take Mary home as your wife, because what is conceived in her is from the Holy Spirit.
She will give birth to a son, and you are to give him the name Jesus because he will save his people from their sins."

. . . When Joseph woke up, he did what the angel of the Lord had commanded him and took Mary home as his wife.

(JOSEPH)

I was torn apart when I learned Mary was with child.
My head told me she had sinned gravely,
but my heart held only grace for her.
I tossed in my bed that night, so sad and confused,
but through the wildness of my dreams
this message came so clear . . .

The Son of God, somehow born of a woman—my future wife!

I have no idea what tomorrow holds,
but I will trust God for this moment.
And even if the whole world doubts,
I will cling to His incredible promise
and protect Mary with all my strength.

A CHRISTMAS BLESSING FOR YOU: *Trust*

To trust requires immense courage. It is a bold act to transcend our human desire for control and embrace the unknown. But it's so very worth it.

Like Joseph, may you hold tight to all God's promises, even—or especially—on the darkest of nights. May you sense His hand working in the details of your life and rest in the fact that you can always trust His heart.

In those days Caesar Augustus issued a decree that a census should be taken of the entire Roman world . . . And everyone went to their own town to register.

So Joseph also went up from the town of Nazareth in Galilee to Judea, to Bethlehem the town of David . . . He went there to register with Mary, who was pledged to be married to him and was expecting a child.

(JOSEPH)

Why, oh Lord, this journey now? We should be safe at home, not traveling farther and farther away. I see Mary, but a child herself, so small a frame to carry such a burden. And yet she does, day by day, willingly. I may lead, but often it is her faith that shows me the way.

(MARY)

Joseph is quiet, but his eyes speak comfort to my spirit when I look at him. Each step we take toward this new place is a step away from all I have ever known.

When doubt begins to fill my heart, and weariness creeps into my bones, I am reminded that the One who has called us surely shares this journey with us. And because of this, I know somehow we'll be all right.

A CHRISTMAS BLESSING FOR YOU: *Faith*

Life is filled with journeys.

Some are joyful. Others difficult.

But all are a part of the bigger picture

that we cannot yet see . . .

the greater story being written

by the Author of our lives.

No matter where you are today,

may you find purpose on your path,

hope in every step,

and faith that you are right

where you're meant to be.

While they were there, the time came for the baby to be born, and she gave birth to her firstborn, a son. She wrapped him in cloths and placed him in a manger, because there was no guest room available for them.

(JOSEPH)

Are these rough hands all I have to hold you with? These carpenter's hands that know every tool, but know nothing of this soft skin just born into the world.

You are so small, so helpless...and yet you have come to save us all! How can it be that God would entrust his most precious gift to Mary and me? The Messiah! Somehow we'll call you Savior, and we'll also call you Son.

(MARY)

Oh, Child. My heart could burst with love. The pain of a moment ago has gone and joy takes my breath away. You are here—no longer within, and yet somehow forever and ever a part of me.

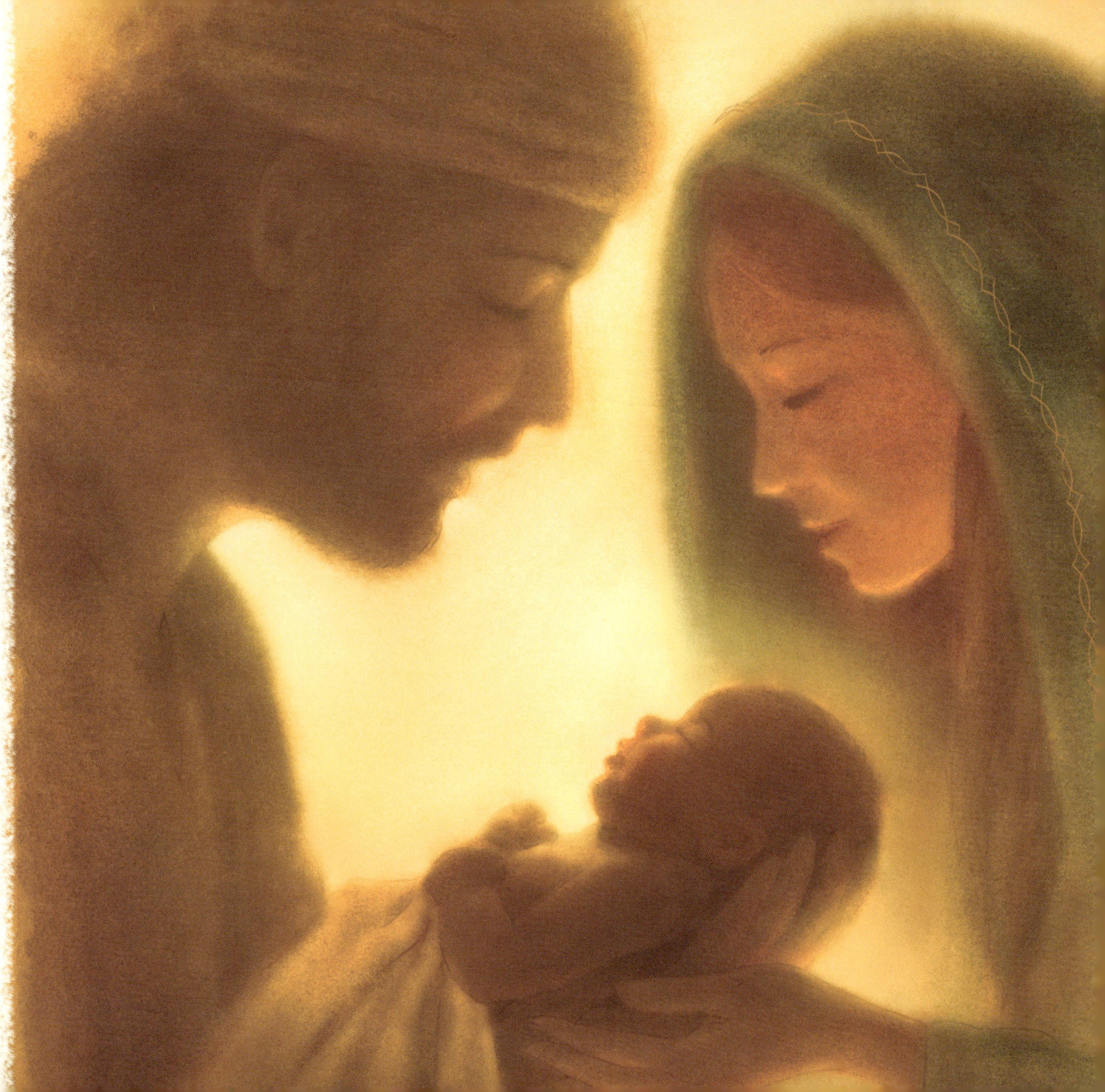

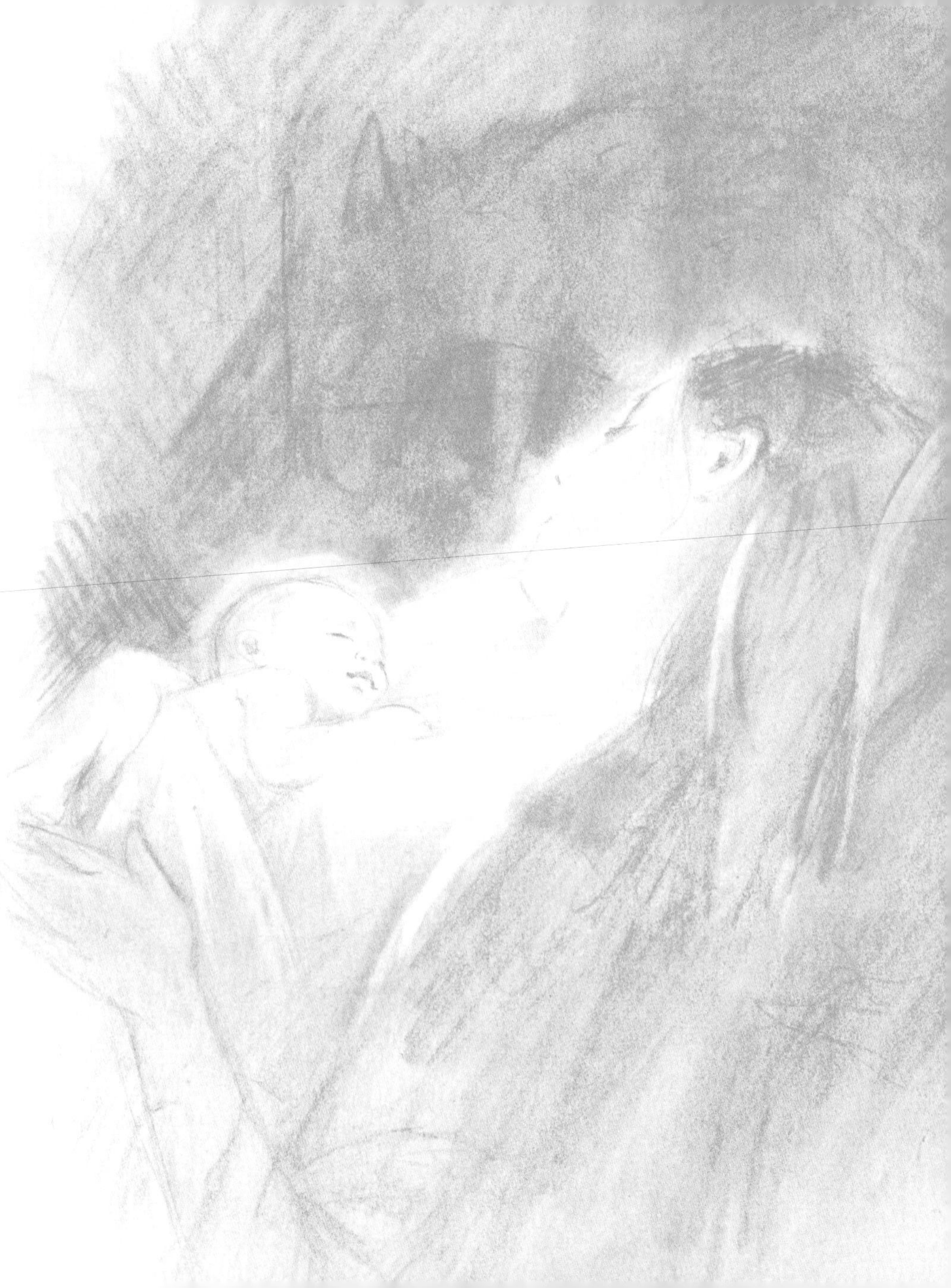

A CHRISTMAS BLESSING FOR YOU: *Love*

To truly love another
is to touch the heart of God,
for love is why He came
to live among us.

He knows we need a love
that will always be a part of us,
that will never let us go.

May you love and be loved
as deeply as God loves you.
And in this, may you discover
the beautiful heart of Jesus living in you
and in those you meet . . .
sometimes in the most unexpected places.

And there were shepherds living out in the fields nearby, keeping watch over their flock at night. An angel of the Lord appeared to them, and the glory of the Lord shone around them, and they were terrified.

But the angel said to them, *"Do not be afraid.*

I bring you good news that will cause great joy for all the people.

Today in the town of David a Savior has been born to you;

he is the Messiah, the Lord. This will be a sign to you:

You will find a baby wrapped in cloths and lying in a manger."

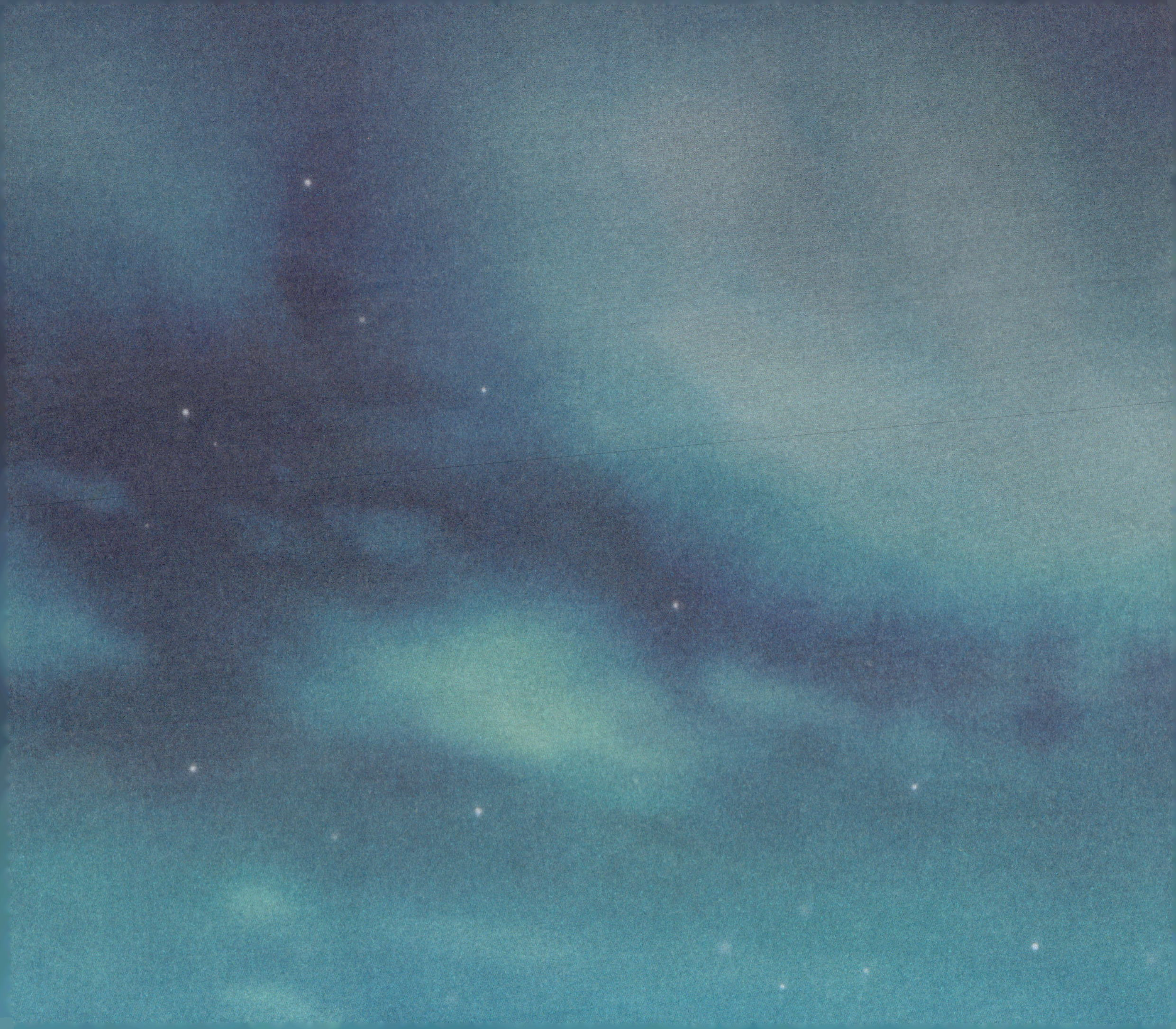

Suddenly, a great company of the heavenly host appeared with the angel, praising God and saying, *"Glory to God in the highest heaven, and on earth peace to those on whom his favor rests."*

When the angels had left them and gone into heaven, the shepherds said to one another, *"Let's go to Bethlehem and see this thing that has happened, which the Lord has told us about."*

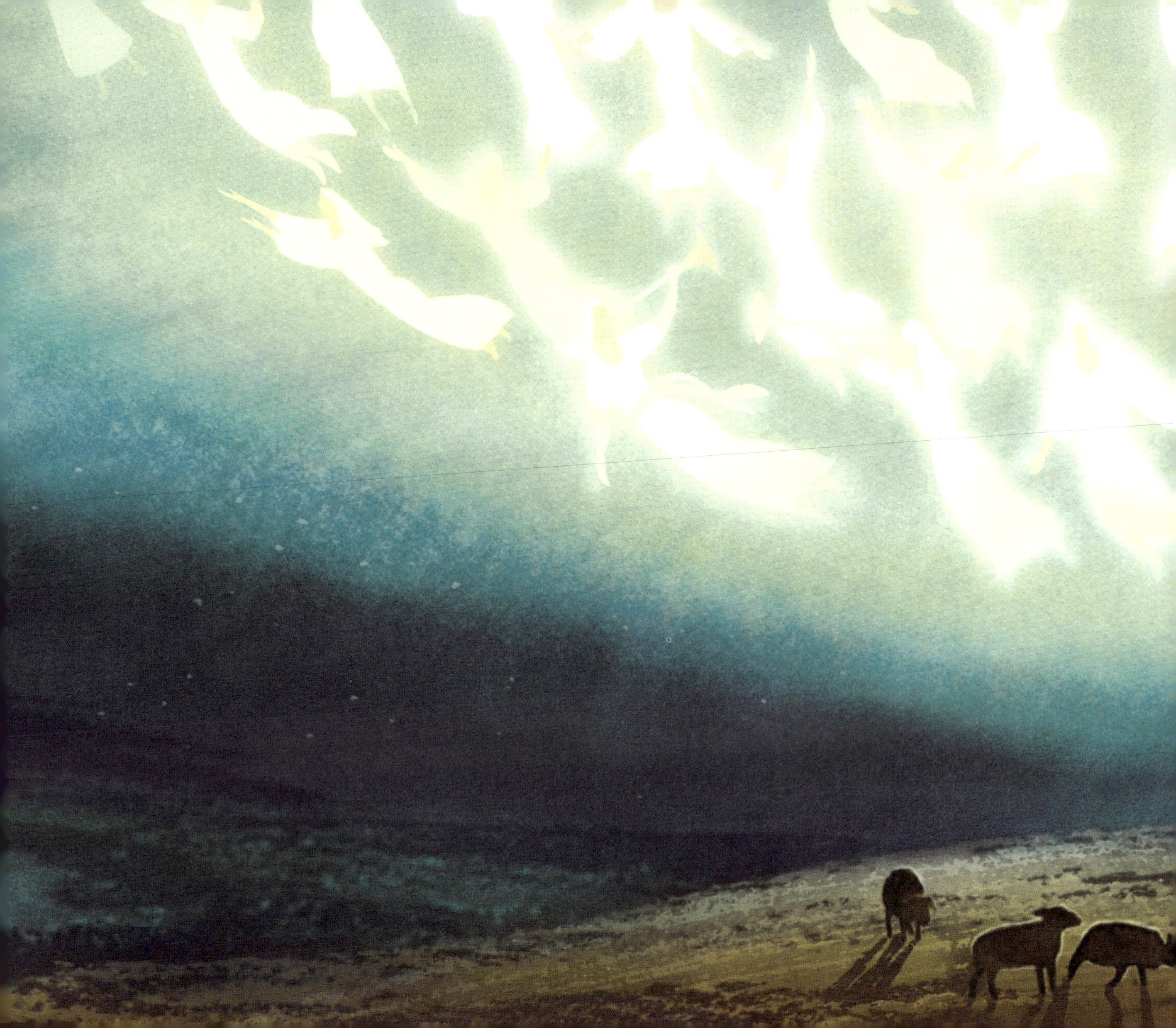

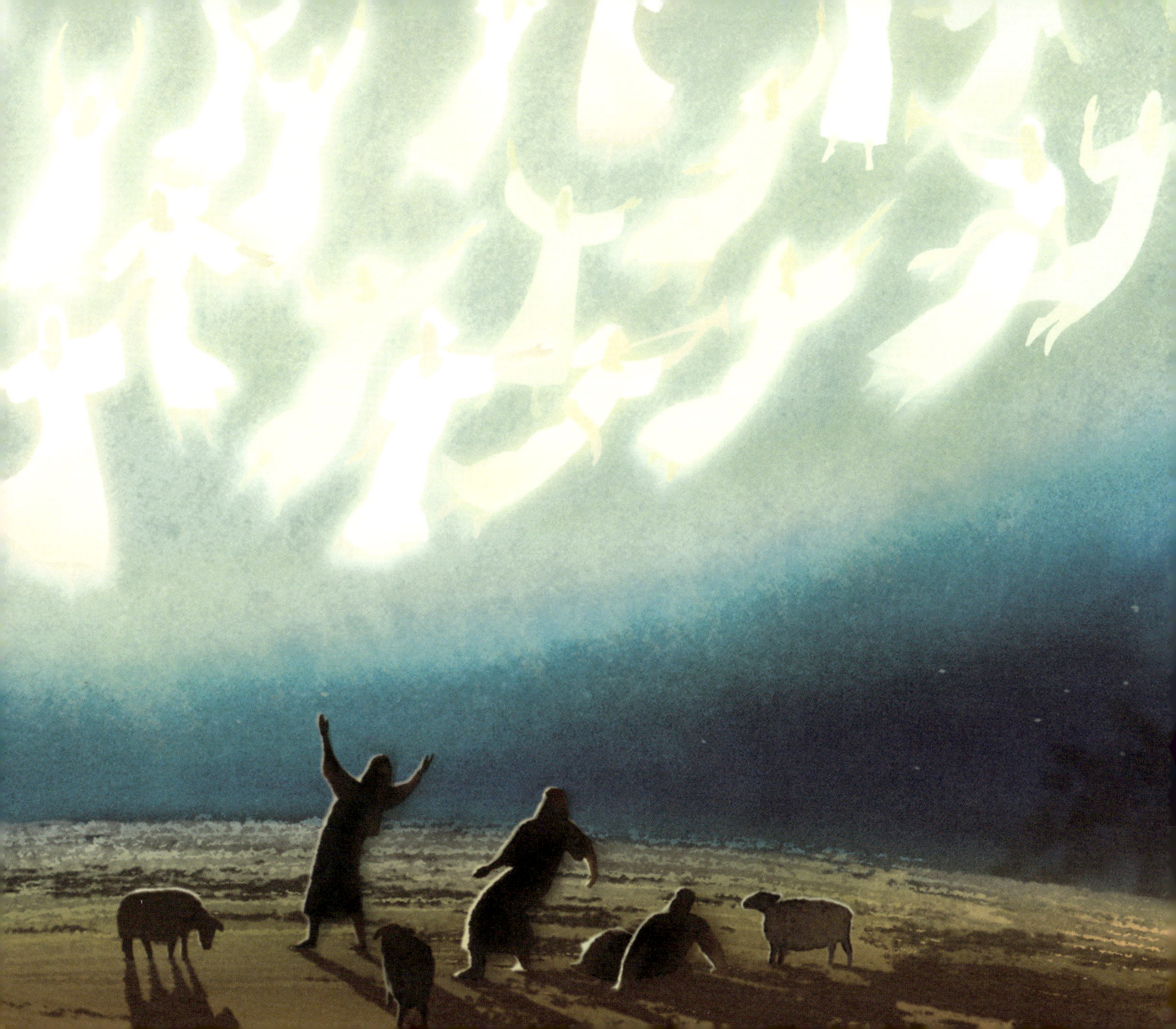

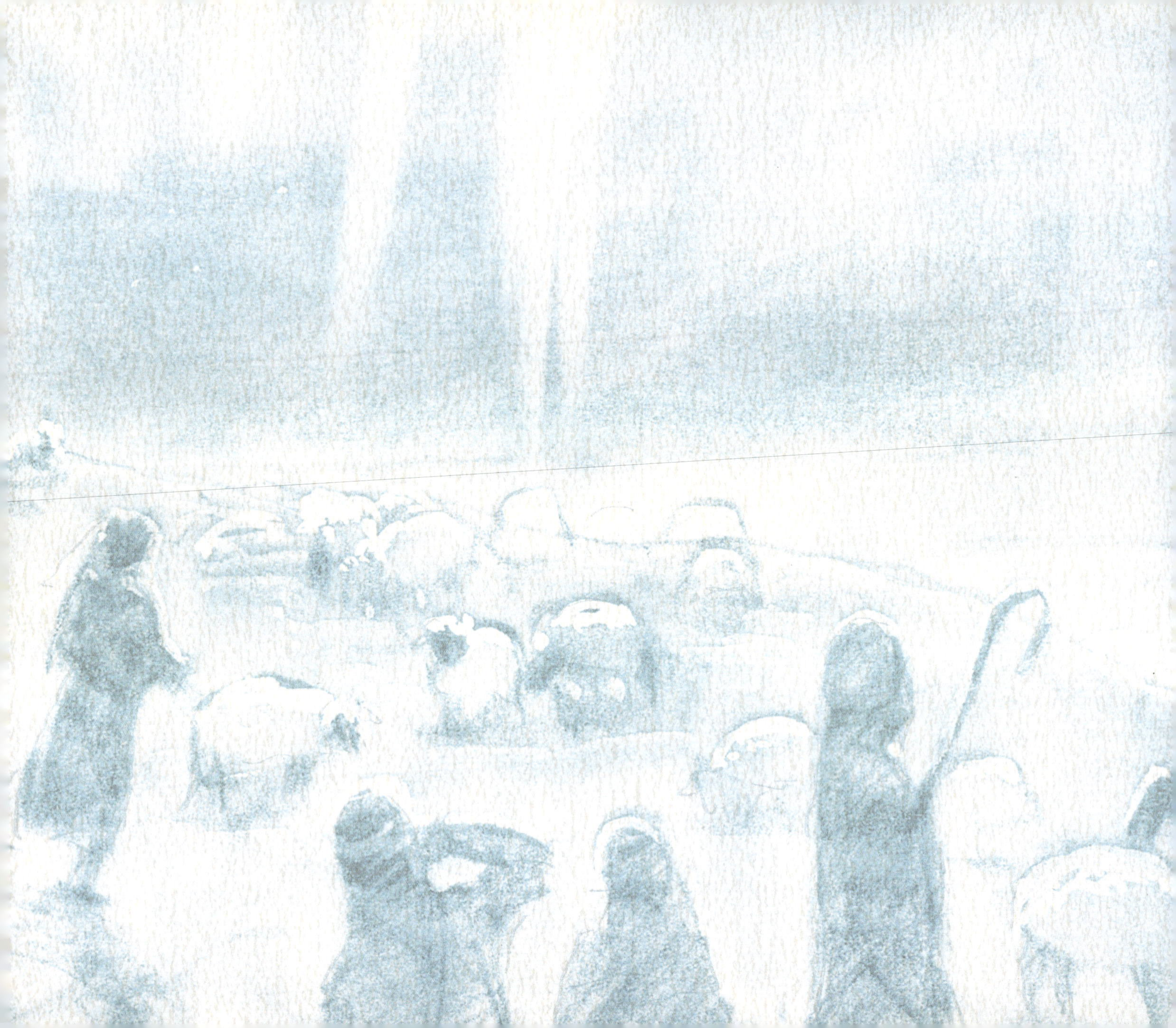

A CHRISTMAS BLESSING FOR YOU: Wonder

When we are young, life is a wonder.
It's full of discovery, adventure, possibility.

Then, we grow up, and somehow
the little everyday things
that don't matter so much
begin to steal our attention away
from the greater things that do.

Wishing you those big moments
of shepherd-like awe again—
beautiful experiences
and unexpected blessings
that give you pause to take in
all of life's wonder again.

The shepherds hurried off and found Mary and Joseph, and the baby, who was lying in a manger.

When they had seen him, they spread the word concerning what had been told them about this child, and all who heard it were amazed at what the shepherds said to them.

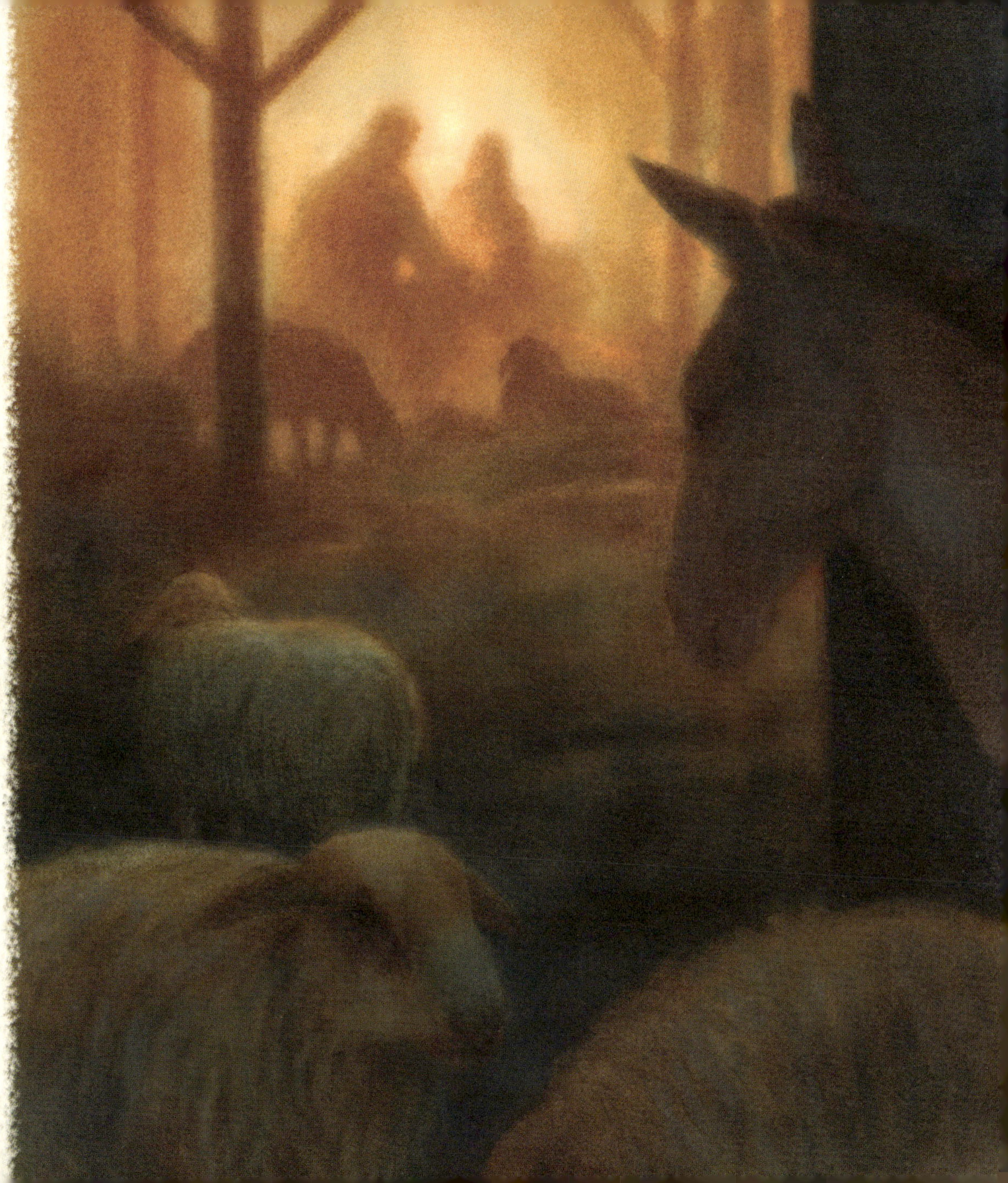

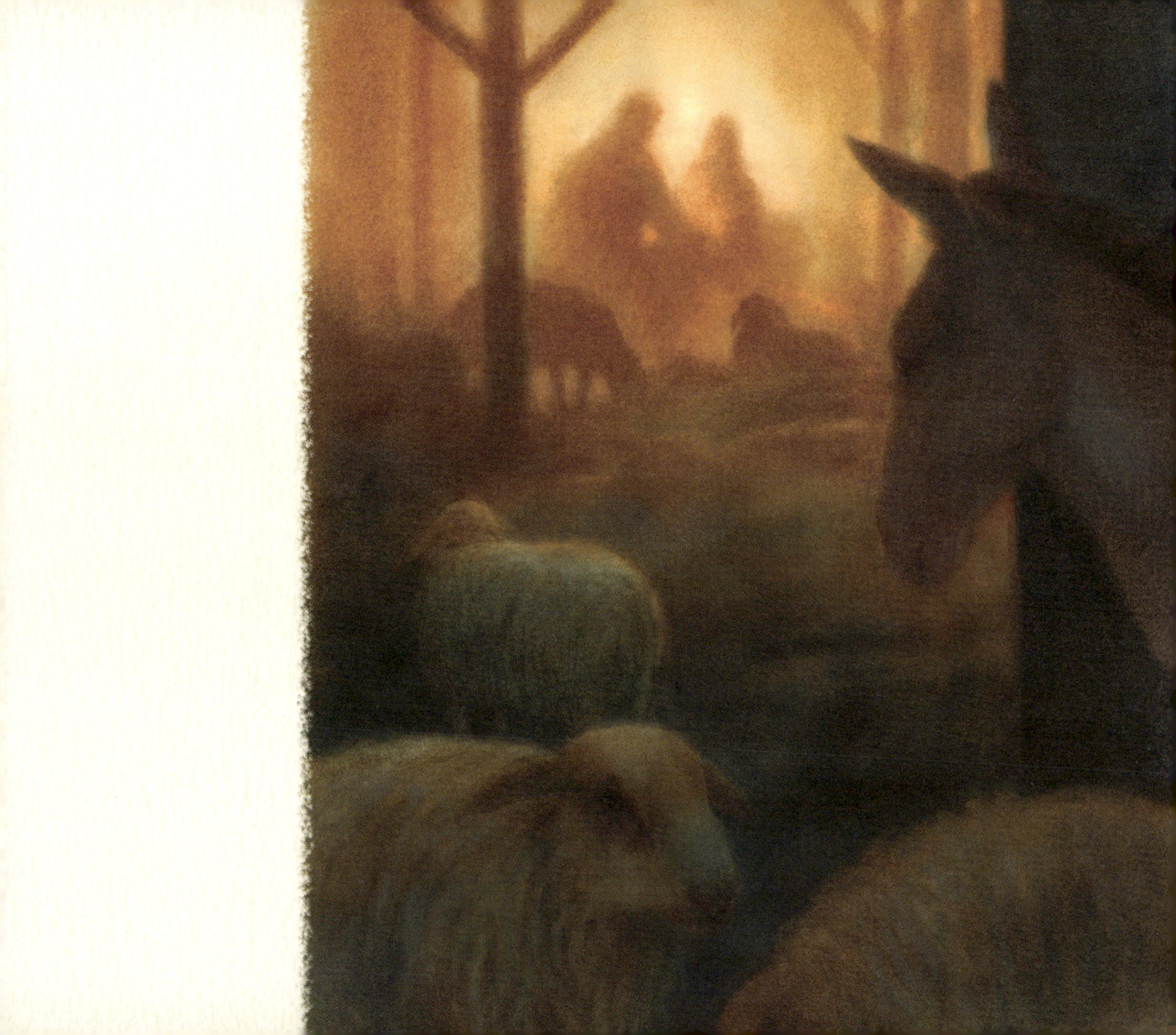

(SHEPHERD)

We were like children when we left that place.
Grown men, singing, dancing for joy!

Even now I wonder, "Why us?" Why not men of importance?
Good men. Religious men. Only God knows, but I am so grateful.

I will return to the fields, but I will never be the same.
This ordinary work is somehow made holy to me now.

My purpose is clear: to honor my Lord in everything I do.

A Christmas Blessing for You: Gratitude

To live gratefully is to find
joy in everyday life.
It is about savoring moments,
great and small,
and opening our hearts
with a great big "thank you,"
to the Creator of all those moments.

Wishing you the joy
of living with a grateful heart each day.
May life continue to bring you
reasons to smile,
blessings to count,
and times when God's goodness
simply takes your breath away.

Mary treasured up all these things and pondered them in her heart.

(MARY)

My baby boy,
your light already shines,
and soon the whole world
will know your presence.
But here we are
tucked away for a moment
to be still and enjoy.
There is so much to feel, to remember,
to treasure forever.
I have no words, only such wonder,
such peace, such love.

A CHRISTMAS BLESSING FOR YOU: *Time to cherish*

Sometimes, in our effort to do and see and be it all, life becomes a nonstop rush. The idea of slowing down seems preposterous, impossible.

Yet deep down we know if we don't pause to rest and reflect, we will one day find ourselves wondering what it all meant.

Wishing you little reminders to slow down and cherish each day in your own special ways.
Like Mary, may your heart be filled with treasured moments that last a lifetime.

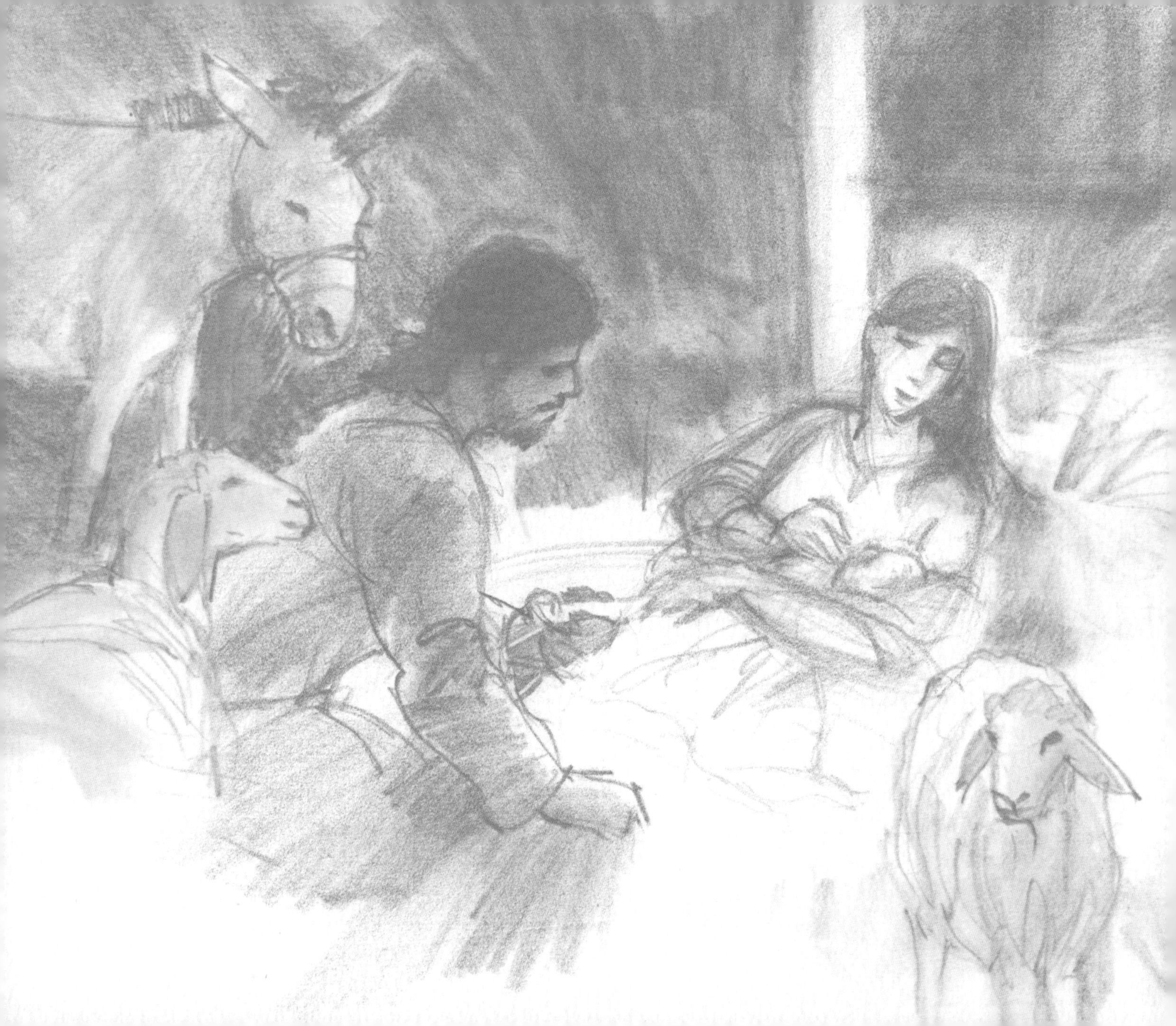

After Jesus was born in Bethlehem in Judea . . . Magi from the east came to Jerusalem and asked, "Where is the one who has been born king of the Jews? We saw his star when it rose and have come to worship him."

When King Herod heard this he was disturbed, and all Jerusalem with him. When he had called together all the people's chief priests and teachers of the law, he asked them where the Messiah was to be born. "In Bethlehem in Judea," they replied, "for this is what the prophet has written."

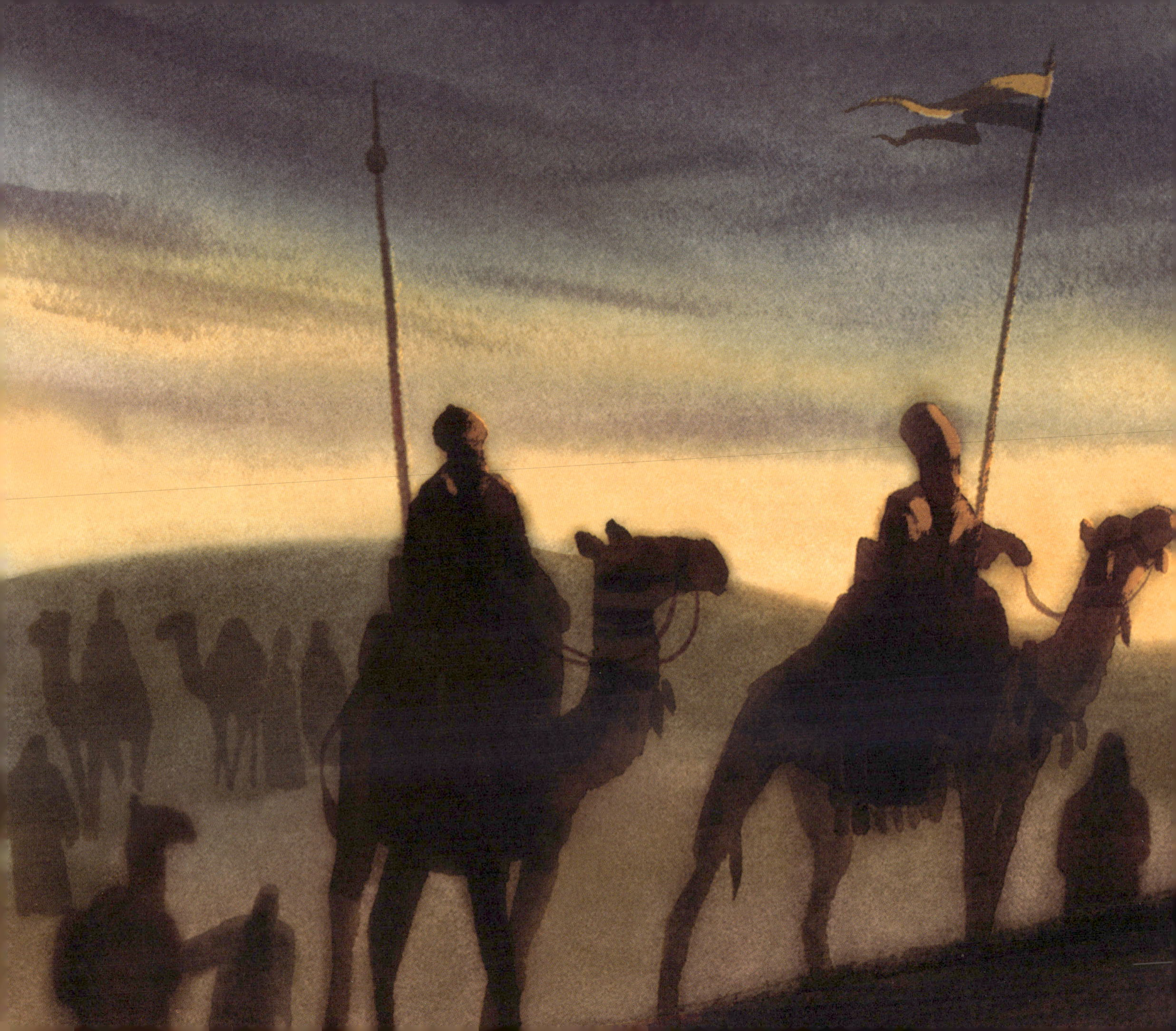

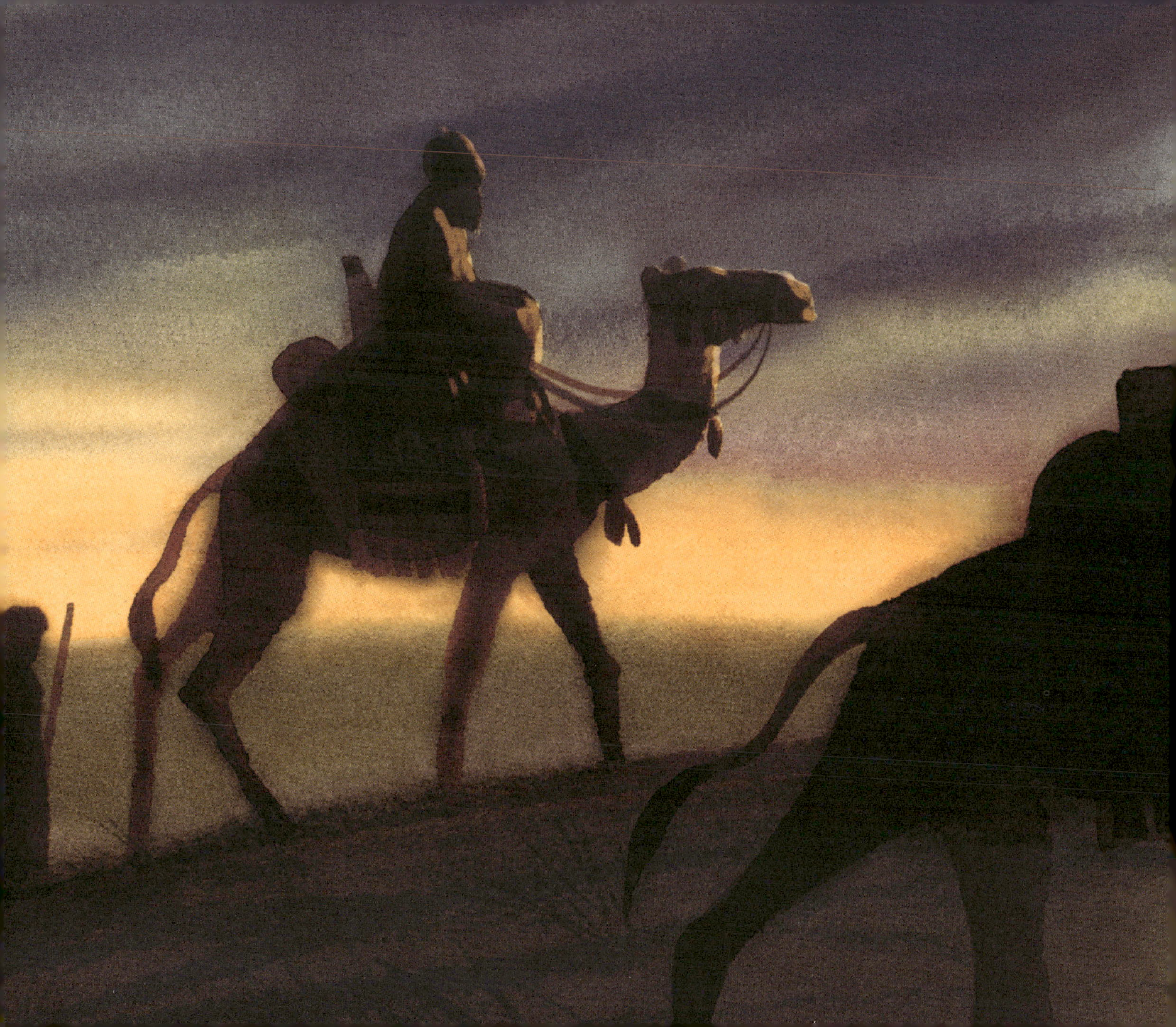

Then Herod called the Magi secretly and found out from them the exact time the star had appeared. He sent them to Bethlehem and said, *"Go and search carefully for the child. As soon as you find him, report to me, so that I, too, may go and worship him."*

After they had heard the king, they went on their way, and the star they had seen when it rose went ahead of them until it stopped over the place where the child was.

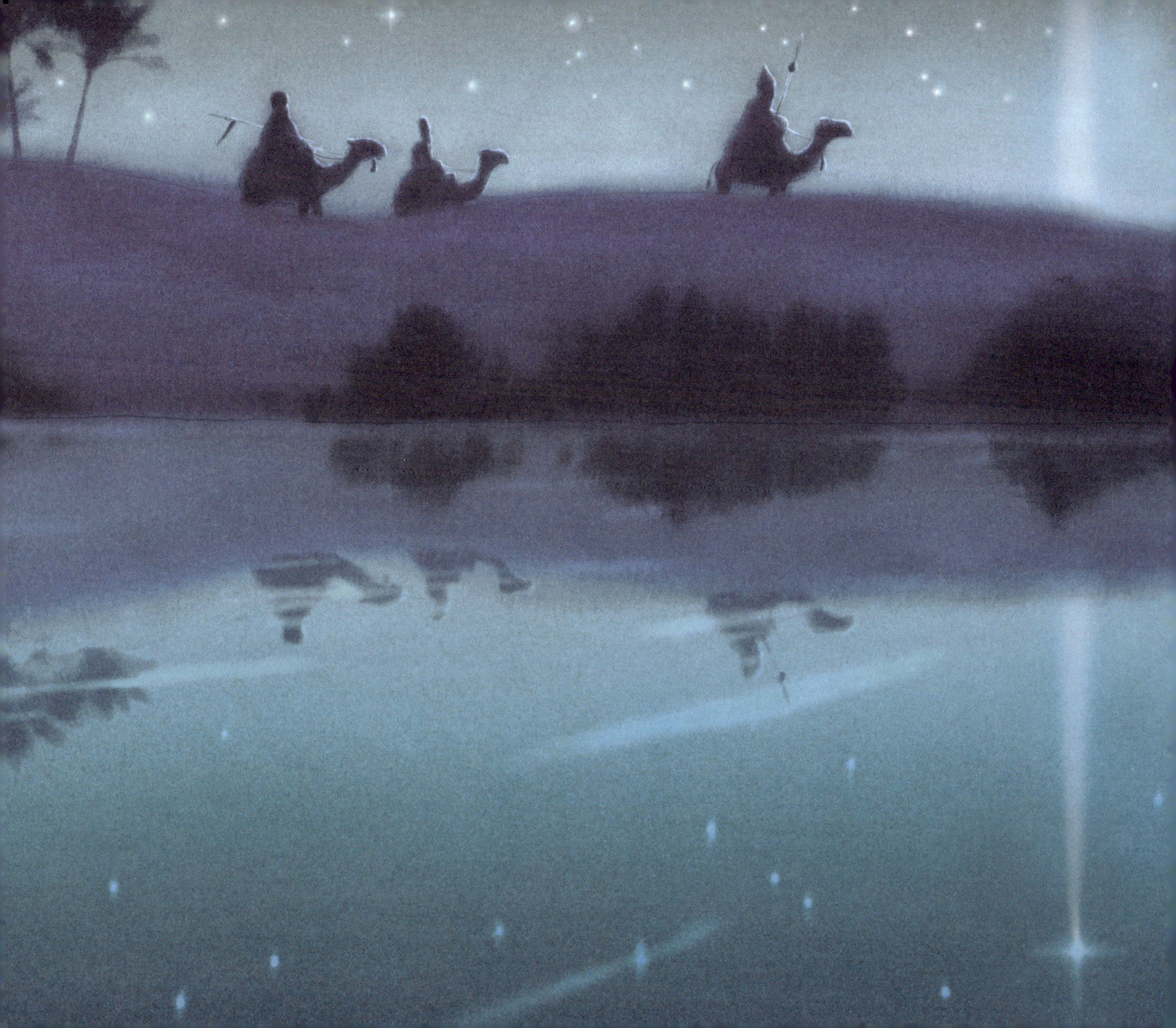

When they saw the star, they were overjoyed.

{MAGI}

Guiding light, so bright and true...
With each step, we are nearer to God.
The mission of a lifetime, no, a thousand lifetimes...
I've never known such joy.

Will men one day hear the story of this star
and marvel at the wondrous works of God?
Or will they scorn us for giving all we had
to chase a dream... a myth... a legend?

I know this to be true: The child we seek
is worth more than all the treasures I possess,
and I would follow countless stars
to find the one that might lead me to his side.

A CHRISTMAS BLESSING FOR YOU: *Joy*

True joy is a blessing

that comes in many forms.

And the more we seek

Christ's presence in our lives,

the more happiness we discover

along the way.

Wishing you a life full of joy—

the quiet kind to sustain you,

the blissful kind to delight you,

and the eternal kind to assure you

that no matter what life brings,

God is always up to something wonderful.

On approaching, the Magi saw the child with his mother Mary, and they bowed down and worshiped him. Then they opened their treasures and presented him with gifts of gold, frankincense, and myrrh.

And having been warned in a dream not to go back to Herod, they returned to their country by another route.

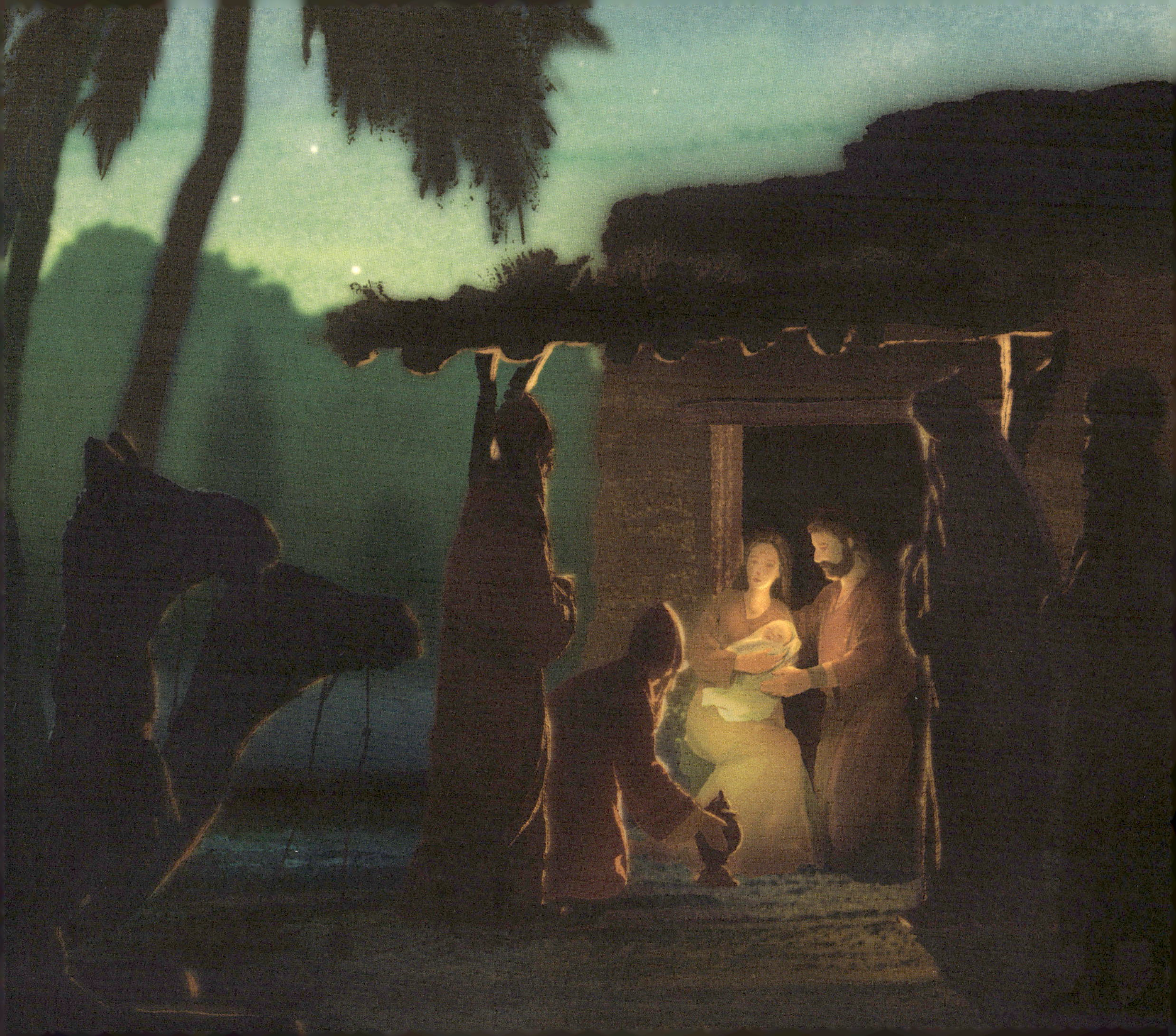

A CHRISTMAS BLESSING FOR YOU: *Hope*

Hope is the whisper of God in every soul
that tells us all will be well.
It's a light in the dark in uncertain times
and a joyful companion on ordinary days.

Wishing you the hope that Jesus represents,
hope for every day and every journey.
May it comfort you, assure you, transform
you, and lead you boldly
into all God has planned for your life.

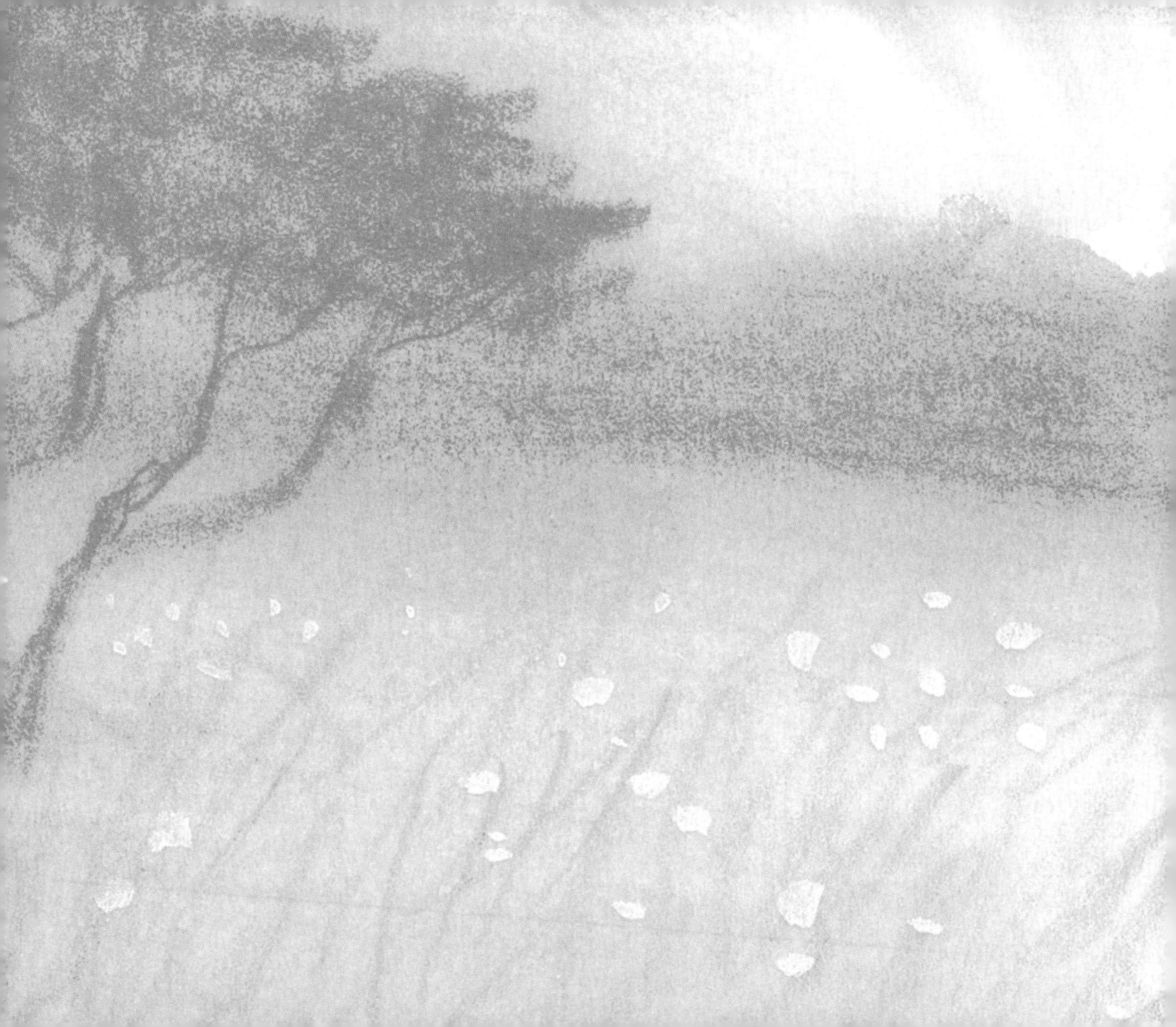

THE PEOPLE WALKING IN DARKNESS HAVE SEEN A GREAT LIGHT;
ON THOSE LIVING IN THE LAND OF DEEP DARKNESS A LIGHT HAS DAWNED.

FOR TO US A CHILD IS BORN, TO US A SON IS GIVEN,
AND THE GOVERNMENT WILL BE ON HIS SHOULDERS.

AND HE WILL BE CALLED WONDERFUL COUNSELOR,
MIGHTY GOD, EVERLASTING FATHER, PRINCE OF PEACE.

– Isaiah 9:2, 6

If you have enjoyed this book or it has touched your life in some way, we would love to hear from you.

PLEASE SEND YOUR COMMENTS TO:
Hallmark Book Feedback
P.O. Box 419034
Mail Drop 100
Kansas City, MO 64141

Or e-mail us at:
booknotes@hallmark.com